OUTSIDERS by galerie objet trouvé

COLLECTION DIRECTOR christian berst (galerie objet trouvé, paris, france)
DESIGN milarépa bacot (iconofolio, paris, france)
PUBLISHER iconofolio (paris, france)

1 — Hans Krüsi

published in collaboration with Andrew Edlin Gallery

TEXT Edward M. Gómez

PHOTOGRAPHS Mario del Curto
from *Les Clandestins sous le vent de l'art brut*, Collection de l'Art Brut, Lausanne, 2000

a co-publishing iconofolio / objet trouvé

www.objet-trouve.com | 16 rue Daval 75011 Paris France
www.edlingallery.com | 529 West 20th Street New York NY 10011 USA
www.iconofolio.com | 23 rue Tourlaque 75018 Paris France

© iconofolio, 2006 — all rights reserved for all countries
copyright : Mario del Curto pp. 3, 6, 59, 60, 63 | Collection de l'Art Brut - Lausanne, photo: Claude Bornand pp. 34-35, 36-37, 39 | Kunstmuseum des Kantons Thurgau pp. 26-27, 32-33, 46 | Eveline Hoster Meeuwse p. 64 | translated from english by Anne-Laure Lackova

isbn 2-35237-009-4

hans krüsi

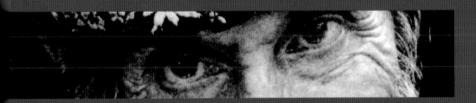

edward m. gómez

*icono*folio

the "nothing" who became a "something"
le « rien » qui est devenu « quelque chose »

Hans Krüsi was born in Zürich in 1920 and died in St. Gallen in 1995. Like his compatriots Adolf Wölfi (1864-1930), Heinrich Anton Müller (1869-1930) and Aloïse (1886-1964), Krüsi is one of several remarkable talents from Switzerland who have earned lasting places in the world of art brut and outsider art.

Krüsi grew up and lived most of his life in or near St. Gallen, in northeastern Switzerland. As a child, he was brought up by foster parents; later, he was sent

Hans Krüsi est né à Zürich en 1920 et mort à Saint-Gall en 1995. Comme ses compatriotes Adolf Wölfi (1864-1930), Heinrich Anton Müller (1869-1930) et Aloïse (1886-1964), Krüsi fait partie de ces talentueux artistes suisses qui bénéficient d'une reconnaissance établie dans le monde de l'art brut et outsider.

Krüsi a grandi et vécu la majeure partie de sa vie à Saint-Gall ou alentour (au nord-est de la Suisse). Élevé par des parents adoptifs avant d'être en-

to an orphanage. Krüsi received only an elementary-school education and did not enjoy a happy childhood. His big desire was to become a professional gardener but he never received formal training in this field.

A gaunt, eccentric loner, Krüsi was poor and lived in run-down buildings in the St. Gallen area. Eventually he began commuting by train to Zürich to sell flowers on the Bahnhofstrasse, one of the most luxurious shopping streets in Europe. In the late 1970s, when he was in his fifties, he began making little paintings on postcard-size scraps of paper or cardboard, which he offered for sale along with bouquets of flowers.

Krüsi's big turn of fate came in 1980, when a representative from Galerie Bu-

voyé dans un orphelinat, il n'est pas allé plus loin que l'école primaire et n'a jamais pu suivre de formation pour devenir jardinier comme il le désirait. Il n'eut pas une enfance heureuse.

Excentrique, ce solitaire au physique émacié était pauvre et vivait dans des bâtiments délabrés aux environs de Saint-Gall. Puis, un jour, il se mit à faire la navette en train jusqu'à Zürich pour y vendre des fleurs sur la Bahnhofstrasse, l'une des rues commerçantes les plus luxueuses d'Europe. À la fin des années 1970, à la cinquantaine, il commença à faire des petites peintures sur des morceaux de papier ou de carton de la taille d'une carte postale, qu'il se mit à vendre avec ses bouquets de fleurs.

En 1980 le destin de Krüsi change totalement quand la galerie *Buchmann*, à

chmann, in St. Gallen, became interested in his paintings and presented them in a solo show the following year. Krüsi was delighted to be taken seriously as an artist and to see his creations sell for more than a few francs apiece. With their vivid colors and energetic brushstrokes, Krüsi's paintings seemed to share something of an expressionist artist's impulsive sensibility.

Around this time, Krüsi's home and studio were located on the top floor of a mostly abandoned building. He shared the space with the many pigeons that flew in and perched among his paintings, wooden sculptures, boxes of photographs and other odds and ends. Among his treasures in this wall-to-wall ocean of clutter: a collection of old cameras and tape recorders that he used to record the sights

Saint-Gall, s'intéresse à ses peintures et les présente lors d'une exposition personnelle l'année suivante. Krüsi est ravi d'être reconnu en tant qu'artiste et de voir ses œuvres se vendre plus de quelques francs la pièce. Avec leurs couleurs vives et leurs coups de pinceaux énergiques, les peintures de Krüsi se rapprochent de la sensibilité impulsive des expressionnistes.

A cette époque, Krüsi logeait et travaillait au dernier étage d'un bâtiment quasiment abandonné. Il partageait les lieux avec de nombreux pigeons qui allaient et venaient dans son studio et se perchaient sur ses peintures, ses sculptures en bois, ses boîtes de photographies ou autres objets épars. Coincée entre quatre murs, parmi ses trésors cachés dans cet immense fatras : une collection de vieux ap-

and sounds of the Swiss countryside that he loved—cows, goats, trees, villagers in traditional folk costumes, farmhouses, the ringing of church bells and the songs of the birds.

What others regarded as junk, Krüsi viewed as precious raw material for future art projects. He painted on shopping bags, cardboard portfolios (for holding drawings), paper napkins and wooden boards. He once glued together dozens of cardboard milk cartons in a grid to create a single large, wide painting surface.

Krüsi savored the creative process and was a tireless experimenter. He used collage techniques and also spray-painted over real fern leaves to create decorative patterns on cardboard or paper. Often he placed

pareils photos et de magnétophones qu'il utilisait pour conserver les images et les sons de la campagne suisse qu'il aimait tant – vaches, chèvres, arbres, villageois dans leurs costumes traditionnels, fermes, son de cloche des églises et chant des oiseaux.

Ce que les autres voyaient comme des déchets, Krüsi les considérait comme une matière première précieuse pour de futurs projets artistiques. Il a peint sur des sacs à provisions, des cartons à dessins, des serviettes en papier et des planches. Il a même assemblé des douzaines de cartons de lait pour créer une large surface à peindre.

Expérimentateur infatigable, Krüsi savourait le processus de création. Adepte des collages, il utilisait aussi la peinture en bombe pour réaliser

colors on his painting surface in what appeared to be a random manner. Later he would pick out shapes from these color compositions, shapes that suggested the forms of human faces, trees or animals. He highlighted these forms with bold, black outlines.

Krüsi took pleasure and pride in his identity as an artist. This strong sense of himself as a maker and purveyor of culture can be seen in the fact that, on his printed business cards, he identified himself as an "art painter." Clearly, his flower-selling days were over.

Like all genuine artists, Krüsi observed the world and interpreted his findings in and through his art. He constantly made drawings in notebooks, on scraps of paper and especially on

des pochoirs à base de feuilles de fougères. Souvent il posait, apparemment au hasard, des couleurs sur la surface. Plus tard il choisirait dans ces compositions colorées des formes suggérant des visages, des arbres ou des animaux. Enfin, il les soulignerait de larges traits noirs.

Krüsi était heureux et fier de son identité d'artiste. Il avait une conscience aigüe de lui-même en tant qu'artisan et pourvoyeur de culture : sur ses cartes de visite imprimées il se présentait comme « un peintre d'art ». L'époque des marchés aux fleurs était définitivement révolue.

Comme tous les véritables artistes, Krüsi a observé le monde et retranscrit ses découvertes dans et par son

ordinary restaurant napkins. He drew on napkins with felt-tip pens and took pleasure in the way the delicate paper absorbed the ink. He liked to unfold a decorated napkin and examine the multiple versions of the same image that appeared in the four quadrants of the thin, porous paper.

From the time of his 1981 Galerie Buchmann show until his death, Krüsi showed his art in numerous one-person exhibitions in commercial galleries in Switzerland. In 1990, on the occasion of his 70th birthday, he was honored with retrospective exhibitions of his work at the Museum im Lagerhaus in St. Gallen, an institution that specializes in the work of self-taught artists, and at the *Collection de l'Art Brut* in Lausanne.

oeuvre. Il faisait constamment des dessins sur des calepins, des morceaux de papier et en particulier sur de simples serviettes de restaurant. Il y dessinait avec des feutres et prenait plaisir à regarder le papier absorber l'encre. Il aimait déplier une serviette ainsi décorée et examiner la même image démultipliée qui apparaissait aux quatre coins.

Depuis son exposition à la galerie *Buchmann* en 1981 jusqu'à sa mort, Krüsi connut de nombreuses expositions personnelles dans des galeries suisses. En 1990, à l'occasion de son 70ème anniversaire, le musée *Im Lagerhaus* de Saint-Gall, dédié au travail d'artistes autodidactes, et la *Collection de l'Art Brut* à Lausanne lui ont rendu hommage en organisant une rétrospective.

"Even a nothing can become a something" Krüsi once said proudly, reflecting on his experiences in life.

After he died, the artist's unsold artworks, sketchbooks, photographs and sound recordings were acquired by the *Kunstmuseum des Kantons Thurgau* in the town of Warth, in northeastern Switzerland. Although Krüsi was not personally associated with the canton of Thurgau during his lifetime, the museum in Warth had a well-established, permanent collection of Swiss folk art and art made by self-taught artists. It provided an interesting and relevant context in which to organize, study and display Krüsi's work. To date, the *Kunstmuseum des Kantons Thurgau* has presented several significant exhibitions that have begun to chart a

« Même un rien peut devenir un quelque chose » a-t-il une fois déclaré, non sans fierté, à propos de son propre parcours.

Après sa mort, ses oeuvres invendues, ses carnets de croquis, ses photographies et ses enregistrements sonores ont été acquis par le *Kunstmuseum des Kantons Thurgau* de la ville de Warth, au nord-est de la Suisse. Même si Krüsi n'a pas été personnellement lié au canton de Thurgovie de son vivant, le musée de Warth possédait déjà une riche collection permanente d'art populaire suisse et d'œuvres d'artistes autodidactes. C'était donc un cadre idéal pour classer, étudier et exposer le travail de Krüsi. Depuis, le *Kunstmuseum des Kantons Thurgau* a organisé plusieurs expositions signi-

course and to set high standards for research about Hans Krüsi's life and multifaceted oeuvre.

The in-depth exploration of Hans Krüsi's art and ideas, and of the world from which they emerged, has only just begun. In addition to the curatorial and conservation work that has been done by the museum in Thurgau, the Swiss filmmaker Andreas Baumberger's 2004 documentary, *Auch ein Esel trägt schwer** (2004), provided a vivid recollection of Krüsi's life and career. In recent years, Andrew Edlin Gallery in New York has introduced North American audiences to the Swiss artist's work, and now, Galerie Objet Trouvé's presentation of a selection of Krüsi's works will help focus attention on his art in one of Europe's most important cultural centers.

ficatives, jetant les bases pour une étude sur la vie et l'œuvre complexe de Hans Krüsi.

L'exploration en profondeur de l'art et des idées de Hans Krüsi, et du monde dont ils ont émergé, vient à peine de commencer. Outre le travail de conservation fait par le musée de Warth, le documentaire du cinéaste suisse Andreas Baumberger, *Auch ein Esel trägt schwer** (2004), offre un témoignage vivant de la vie et de la carrière de Krüsi. Depuis quelques années, la galerie Andrew Edlin à New York a considérablement élargi l'audience de l'artiste suisse auprès du public nord-américain. La Galerie Objet Trouvé, à Paris, qui présente une sélection des travaux de Krüsi, permettra enfin de mettre en lumière cet art au sein d'un des plus importants centres culturels européens.

* Even a donkey carries its burden

* Même un âne porte sa charge

Through initiatives such as these, Krüsi's art may come to occupy a more visible and honored place in the international canon of self-taught artists' works. It certainly deserves to find a wider audience, both within this specialized field and far beyond it, too.

Edward M. Gómez

Edward Madrid Gómez is a critic and contributor to various publications in the United States, Europe, Japan and Mexico, including the New York Times, the San Francisco Chronicle (S.F. Gate), Art in America, ARTnews, Art + Auction, Art & Antiques and Fahrenheit. He is the U.S. contributing editor of Raw Vision, the London-based, international magazine about outsider and visionary art. He is a co-author of Yes: Yoko Ono (Harry N. Abrams, 2000) and The Art of Adolf Wölfi: St. Adolf—Giant—Creation (American Folk Art Museum/Princeton Universty Press, 2003).

De telles initiatives permettront à Krüsi d'occuper une place plus visible et reconnue dans le cercle international des artistes autodidactes. Il mérite certainement de trouver un public plus large, dans le champ spécialisé de l'art brut et au-delà.

Edward M. Gómez

Edward Madrid Gómez est critique et correspondant de diverses publications aux Etats-Unis, en Europe, au Japon et au Mexique, dont le New-York Times, San Francisco Chronicle, (S.F. Gate), Art in America, ARTnews, Art + Auction, Art & Antiques et Fahrenheit.. Il est le correspondant nord-américain pour Raw Vision, magazine international basé à Londres, spécialiste de l'outsider art et de l'art visionnaire. Il est coauteur de Yes: Yoko Ono (Harry N. Abrams, 2000) and The Art of Adolf Wölfi: St. Adolf—Giant—Creation (American Folk Art Museum/Princeton Universty Press, 2003).

1977. V.4. HK.

works œuvres

Hs Krüsi 3VI 1991

22

19 Ⅱ 1976   Hs Kr u i

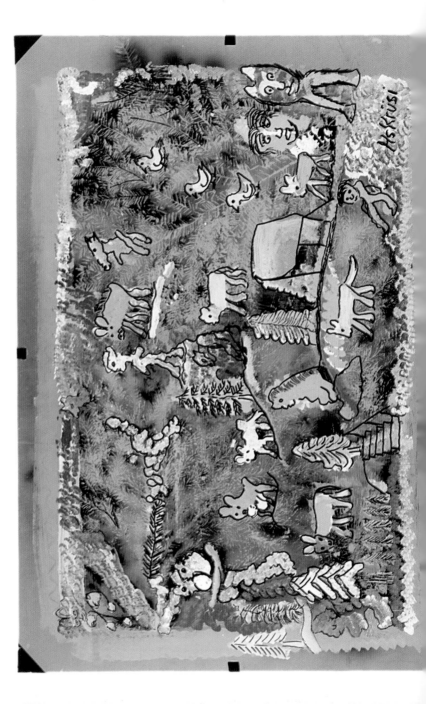

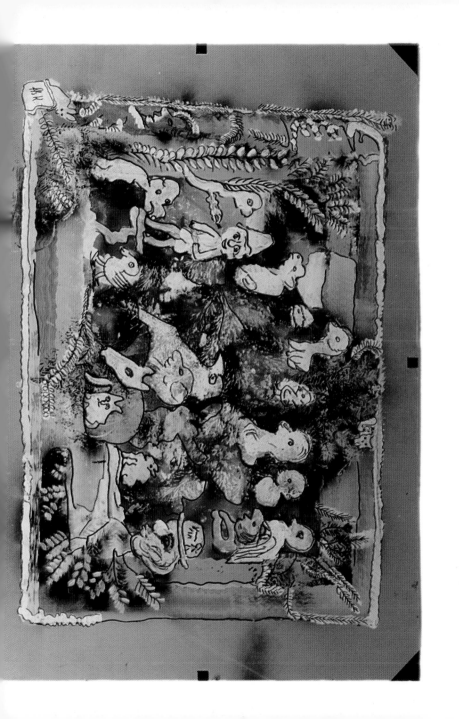

1982.

35

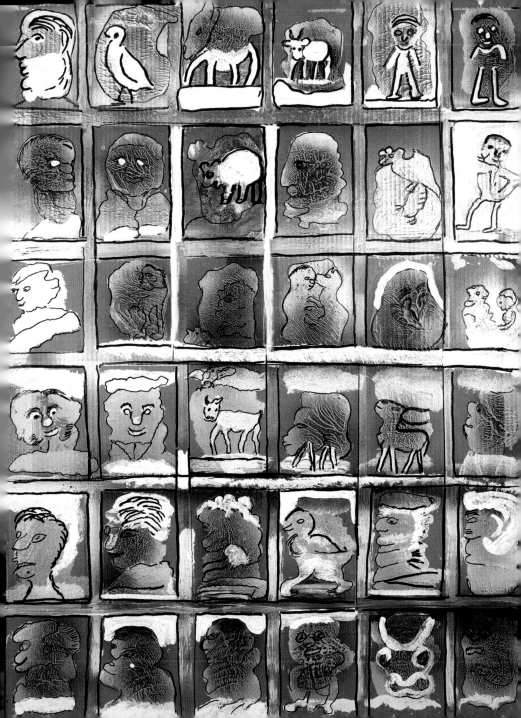

1983   HsK.

1984.   HansKrüsi

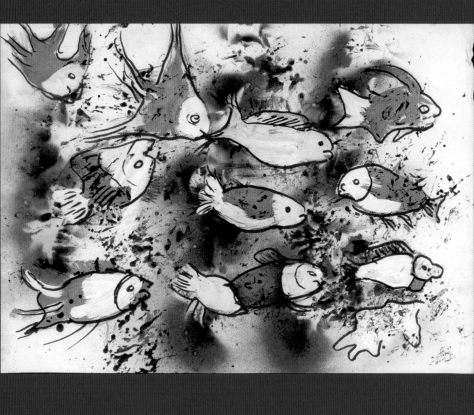

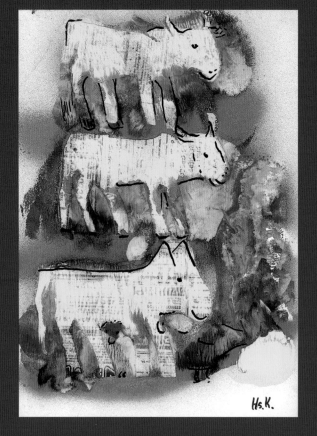

Hs.K.

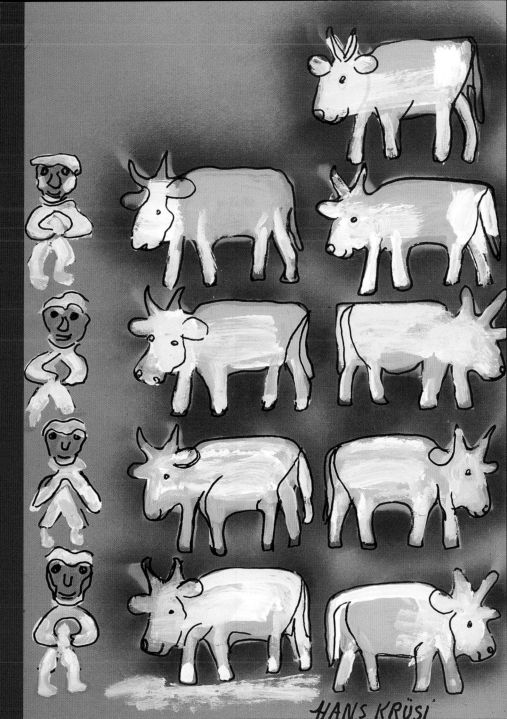

HANS KRÜSI

1968

HK

48

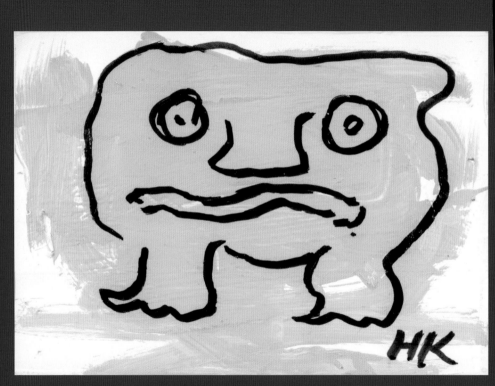

54

1484.   Hs. Krüsi

key légendes

All works are untitled and mixed media on paper (except pp. 4-5, 32-33, 38, 48 on cardboard; pp. 15, 49, 54 mixed media; pp. 28-29, 30-31 on portfolio; pp. 26-27 gouache on box; p. 34 gouache on paper; pp. 36-37 gouache on cartons; p. 39 gouache and argentic color on cardboard).
Toutes les oeuvres sont sans titre et technique mixte sur papier (sauf pp. 4-5, 32-33, 38, 48 sur carton ; pp. 15, 49, 54 technique mixte ; pp. 28-29, 30-31 sur carton à dessin ; pp. 26-27 gouache sur carton d'emballage; p.34 gouache sur papier ; pp. 36-37 gouache sur berlingots ; p. 39 gouache et peinture argentique sur carton).

p. 1	124 x 89 cm (detail - détail)
pp. 4–5	63 x 130 cm, 1980
p. 10	circa 1982 (private collection - collection privée)
p. 15	38 x 38 cm, 1982
p. 18	49 x 77 cm, 1977 (private collection - collection privée)
p. 20	30 x 40 cm
p. 21	30 x 40 cm
p. 22	69 x 99 cm, 1981
p. 23	24 x 34 cm, 1976
pp. 24-25	53 x 79 cm, circa 1981
pp. 26-27	94 x 274 cm, 1981 (*Kunstmuseum des Kantons Thurgau*)
pp. 28-29	124 x 89 cm (side A)
pp. 30-31	124 x 89 cm (side B)
pp. 32-33	70,2 x 101,3 cm, 1983 (*Kunstmuseum des Kantons Thurgau*)
pp. 34-35	70 x 100 cm, 1983 (*Collection de l'Art Brut* - Lausanne; photo: Claude Bornand)
pp. 36-37	51,5 x 79 x 6,5 cm, 1983 (*Collection de l'Art Brut* - Lausanne; photo: Claude Bornand)
p. 38	79 x 109 cm
p. 39	101,5 x 76 x 6,5 cm, 1983 (*Collection de l'Art Brut* - Lausanne; photo: Claude Bornand)
p. 40	46 x 61 cm
p. 41	28 x 35 cm, 1983
p. 42	10 x 15 cm
p. 43	28 x 35 cm, 1984
p. 44	25 x 35 cm
p. 45	28 x 41 cm, 1977
p. 46	41,5 x 29,3 cm (*Kunstmuseum des Kantons Thurgau*)
p. 47	63 x 46 cm, 1986 (private collection - collection privée)
p. 48	77,5 x 54,5 cm, 1968
p. 49	33 x 46 cm
p. 50	35 x 28 cm
p. 51	43 x 30 cm, 1984
p. 52	10 x 15 cm
p. 53	10 x 15 cm
p. 54	38 x 38 cm
p. 55	40 x 29 cm, 1984
p. 56	25 x 35 cm, circa 1977 (private collection - collection privée)

pp. 6, 59, 60, 63	photos by Mario del Curto
	(in *Les Clandestins sous le vent de l'art brut*, Collection de l'Art Brut, Lausanne)
p. 64	photo by Eveline Hoster (*Kunstmuseum des Kantons Thurgau*)
front cover	portait from a photo by Mario del Curto

museum acquisitions
collections publiques

Collection de L'Art Brut, Lausanne (CH)
Irish Museum of Modern Art, Musgrave Kinley Outsider Art Collection, Dublin (IR)
Kunstmuseum Des Kantons Thurgau, Warth (CH)
Kunstmuseum, St. Gallen (CH)
Musée d'art Moderne de Lille-Métropole, Collection l'Aracine (FR)
Museum im Lagerhaus, St. Gallen (CH)

exhibitions expositions

selected solo exhibitions expositions personnelles (sélection)

2006   Galerie Objet Trouvé, Paris (FR)

2005   Kunstmuseum des Kanton Thurgau, Warth (CH)

2002   Andrew Edlin Gallery, New York (US)

2001   Kunstmuseum Des Kantons Thurgau, Warth (CH)
        Volkskundemuseum, Stein (CH)

2000   Galerie Stuker, Zürich (CH)

1996   Chelsea Galerie, Laufen (CH)
        Museum im Lagerhaus, St. Gallen (CH)
        St. Galler Kantonalbank, Herisau (CH)

1995	Galerie Christian Schneeberger, St. Gallen (CH)
	Museum Chasa Jaura, Val Mustair, Valchava (CH)
	Kunstmuseum Des Kantons Thurgau, Warth (CH)

1993	Galerie Die Bühne, Winterhur (CH)
	Galerie Martin Krebs, Bern (CH)

1990	Collection de L'Art Brut, Lausanne (CH)
	Museum im Lagerhaus, St. Gallen (CH)

1986	Galerie Walcheturm, Zürich (CH)
	Kunstmuseum Des Kantons Thurgau, Warth (CH)

| 1985 | Galerie Contemporaine, Carouge-Genf (CH) |

| 1984 | Art Basel, Galerie Contemporaine (CH) |

1981	Galerie Buchmann, St. Gallen (CH)
	Galerie Anton Meier, Genf (CH)
	Galerie Severina Teucher, Zürich (CH)
	Galerie Quadriga Forum, Zürich (CH)

| 1975 | Engros-Blumenhandlung Hans Fischer, St. Gallen (CH) |

selected group exhibitions expositions collectives (sélection)

| 2002 | Irish Museum of Modern Art, Musgrave Kinley Collection, Dublin (IE) |

2000	Galerie Arte Nuova, Flawil (CH)
	Galerie Stuker, Zürich (CH)

| 1997 | Halle Saint-Pierre, Paris (FR) |

| 1995 | Art Brut et Compagnie, Halle Saint-Pierre, Paris (FR) |

| 1988 | Galerie Susi Brunner, Zürich (CH) |

| 1987 | St. Gallen Kunstmuseum, St. Gallen (CH) |

| 1985 | Art Basel, Galerie Susi Brunner (CH) |

bibliography bibliographie

The New York Times, Edward M. Gómez, «A Nothing Who Became Something: an Artist», p. 37 Arts & Leisure section, Sunday, December 1, 2002

Hans Krüsi. Auch ein Nichts Kann Etwas Werden. Kunstmuseum des Kantons Thurgau (8 Apr. - 7 Okt. 2001), Sulgen 2001. Ernst Thoma: Krüsis Konzert, (hrsg. Kunstmuseum des Kantons Thurgau, Dorothee Messmer und Markus Landert) CD Rom, Sulgen 2001.

L'Art Brut. Lucienne Peiry, Flammarion, Paris, 1997 (english edition 2001)

Marco Obrist: Hans Krüsi. In: Biografisches Lexikon der Schweizer Kunst. (Hrsg. Schweizerisches Institut für Kunstwissenschaft SIK) Zürich 1998. Kunstmuseum des Kantons Thurgau, Dorothee Messmer und Markus Landert

Die Servietten des Hans Krüsi (Ausstellungskatalog: St. Gallen, Museum im Lagerhaus. Simone Schaufelberger-Breguet, Peter Schaufelberger-Breguet: Stiftung für schweizerische naive Kunst und art brut, 22. Nov. 1996 - 2.Feb.1997) St. Gallen 1996.

Wandkalender 1996 mit Bildern von Hans Krüsi, Gipf-Oberfrick 1996, Artour Verlag

Peter Killer, Peter Ritter, Rudolf Hanhart: Willkommen im Hühnerstall (catalogue) Bilder und Zeichnungen von Hans Krüsi (Galerie und Edition Buchmann). St. Gallen 1981.

Simone Schaufelberger-Breguet, Elisabeth Grossmann: «Naive Malerei - naiv? Kunst um den Bodensee». 35. Singener Kunstausstellung. (catalogue: Singen, Bürgersaal des Rathauses Singen, 20. Aug. - 12. Sep. 1982) Singen 1982.

Paul-André Jaccard, Heiny Widmer, Beat Wismer: Aargauer Kunsthaus Aarau.

Sammlungskatalog. Band 2. Werke des 20. Jahrhunderts. Von Cuno Amiet bisheute. (Schweizerisches Institut für Kunstwissenschaft. Kataloge Schweizer-Museen und Sammlungen 5/2). Baden 1983.

Pierre Biner, Simon Edelstein: Hans Krüsi - Film. Originalfassungfranzösisch, deutsche Fassung leicht gekürzt. Fernsehen TSR/DRS 1984.

Roland Wälchli / Erika Billeter: Realisten der Sehnsucht. Acht Ostschweizer Künstler (Ausstellungskatalog: Olten, Stadthaus, 18. März - 15. April 1984. Kunstverein Olten) Olten 1984.

Thomas Breymann: L'art brut. Hans Krüsi. In: Josef Wittlich, Willem van Genk, Hans Krüsi et divers autres.(Fascicule 14 der collection de l'art brut) Lausanne 1986.

unb.: In another world - Outsider art from Europe & America. (Ausstellungskatalog Wanderausstellung The South Bank Center, div. britische Städte, Juni 1987 - Mai 1988) London 1987.

Simone Schaufelberger-Breguet: L'Aracine - Musée d'Art Brut. (Sammelkatalog) Neuilly-sur-Marne 1988.

Stiftung für schweizerische naive Kunst und art brut. Die Stiftung stellt ihre Sammlung vor. (Katalog) St. Gallen 1988.

Michel Thévoz u.a.: Neuve Invention. Publication de la Collection de l'Art Brut, Lausanne 1988.

Paolo Bianchi: Bild und Seele - Über Art Brut und Outsider-Kunst. Mit Beiträgen von Simone Schaufelberger-Breguet u.a., Kunstforum International Band 101, Köln 1989.

Michel Thévoz: Art Brut - Kunst jenseits der Kunst. (AT Verlag) Aarau 1990.

Peter Killer, Peter Schaufelberger, Siegfried Kuhn (Fotos), Amelia Magro

(Fotos): Hans Krüsi. Zum 70. Geburtstag von Hans Krüsi. (Säntis Verlag) Urnäsch 1991.

Josef John: Meine Freunde - die ungelernten Meister. Bestaunt - belächelt - verkannt. Wittenbach 1991.

Gottfried Korff: Volkskunst im Wandel. In: Paul Hugger (Hrsg): Handbuch der Schweizerischen Volkskultur. (Offizin Verlag) Zürich 1992. S 1351 - 1373

Ernst Hohl (Hrsg.): Bauernmalerei rund um den Säntis. Mit Beiträgen von Hans Büchler, Hans Hürlemann, Peter Killer und Simone Schaufelberger-Breguet. (Offizin-Verlag) Zürich 1994.

tanghe printing (belgium), 2006